ℒENT and ℰASTER ℳISDOM

—— *from* ——

HENRI J. M. NOUWEN

LENT and EASTER WISDOM
from
HENRI J. M. NOUWEN

Daily Scripture and Prayers Together
With Nouwen's Own Words

Compiled by Judy Bauer

Liguori
LIGUORI, MISSOURI

Imprimi Potest:
Richard Thibodeau, CSsR
Provincial, Denver Province
The Redemptorists

Published by Liguori Publications
Liguori, Missouri

To order, call 800-325-9521
www.liguori.org

Library of Congress Cataloging-in-Publication Data

Nouwen, Henri J. M.
    Lent and Easter wisdom from Henri J. M. Nouwen : daily scriptures and prayers together with Nouwen's own words / compiled by Judy Bauer.—lst ed.
    p. cm.
    ISBN 978-0-7648-1286-6
    1. Lent—Prayer-books and devotions—English. 2. Easter—Prayer-books and devotions—English. 3. Catholic Church—Prayer-books and devotions—English. I. Bauer, Judy, 1941– II. Title.

BX2170.L4N67 2005
242'.34—dc22   2004061639

Scripture citations are taken from the *New Revised Standard Version of the Bible,* copyright 1989 by the Division of Christian Education of the National Council of the Churches of Christ in the USA. All rights reserved. Used with permission.

Acknowledgments of sources of quotations from Henri J. M. Nouwen are listed on pages 113–118.

Liguori Publications, a nonprofit corporation, is an apostolate of the Redemptorists. To learn more about the Redemptorists, visit *Redemptorists.com.*

Printed in the United States of America
17 16 15 14 13 / 11 10 9 8 7
First Edition

Contents

Epigraph

I PRAY THAT WE MAY be found worthy to be cursed, censured, and ground down, and even put to death in the name of Jesus Christ, so long as Christ himself is not put to death in us.

PAULINUS OF NOLA

Introduction

MOST CATHOLICS seem to be aware that the forty-day period be-fore the feast of Easter, Lent—which comes from the Anglo-Saxon word *lencten*, meaning "spring"—is a time marked by particular rituals, such as the reception of ashes on Ash Wednesday or the decision to "give up French fries." Is Lent broader than just these practices that seem to be left over from another era?

A BRIEF HISTORY OF LENT

In the first three centuries of Christian experience, preparation for the Easter feast usually covered a period of one or two days, per-haps a week at the most. Saint Irenaeus of Lyons (ca. AD 140–202) even speaks of a *forty-hour* preparation for Easter.

The first reference to Lent as a period of forty days' prepara-tion occurs in the teachings of the First Council of Nicaea in AD 325. By the end of the fourth century, a Lenten period of forty days was established and accepted.

In its early development, Lent quickly became associated with the sacrament of baptism, since Easter was the great baptismal feast. Those who were preparing to be baptized participated in the season of Lent in preparation for the reception of the sacrament of baptism. Eventually, those who were already baptized considered it important to join these candidates preparing for baptism in their preparations for Easter. The customs and practices of Lent as we know them today soon took hold.

LENT AS A JOURNEY

Lent is often portrayed as a journey, from one point in time to another point in time. The concept of journey is obvious for those experiencing the Rite of Christian Initiation of Adults (RCIA), the program of baptismal preparation conducted in most parishes during the season of Lent.

But Lenten preparation is not limited to those who are preparing to be baptized and join the Church. For many Catholics, Lent is a journey that is measured from Ash Wednesday through Easter Sunday, but, more accurately, Lent is measured from Ash Wednesday to the beginning of the period known as the Triduum.

Triduum begins with the evening Mass of the Lord's Supper on Holy Thursday, reaches its high point in the Easter Vigil on Holy Saturday, and closes with the proclamation of the *Exsultet*, "Rejoice, O Heavenly Powers," during the Mass of Holy Saturday.

By whatever yardstick the journey is measured, it is not only the time that is important but the essential experiences of the journey that are necessary for a full appreciation of what is being celebrated.

The Lenten journey is also a process of spiritual growth and, as such, presumes movement from one state of being to another state. For example, some people may find themselves troubled and anxious at the beginning of Lent as a result of a life choice or an unanswered question, and, at the end of Lent, they may fully expect a sense of conversion, a sense of peace, or perhaps simply understanding and acceptance. Therefore, Lent is a movement from one point of view to another or, perhaps, from one interpretation of life to a different interpretation.

Scripture, psalms, prayers, rituals, practices, and penance are the components of the Lenten journey. Each component, tried and tested by years of tradition, is one of the "engines" that drives the season and which brings the weary spiritual traveler to the joys of Easter.

PENITENTIAL NATURE OF LENT

A popular understanding of Lent is that it is a penitential period of time during which people attempt to become more sensitive to the role of sin in their lives. Lenten sermons will speak of personal sin, coming to an awareness of the sins of others and the effect such sin might have, and, finally, the sin that can be found within our larger society and culture. Awareness of sin, however, is balanced by an emphasis on the love and acceptance that God still has for humanity, despite the sinful condition in which we still find ourselves.

The practice of meditation of the Passion of the Lord, his suffering, and his death is also seen as part of the penitential experience of Lent. There is also a traditional concern for the reception of the sacrament of reconciliation during Lent. Originally, the sacrament of reconciliation was celebrated before Lent began, the penance was imposed on Ash Wednesday, and performed during the entire forty-day period.

SUMMONS TO PENITENTIAL LIVING

"Jesus came to Galilee, proclaiming the good news of God, and saying, 'The time is fulfilled, and the kingdom of God has come near; repent, and believe in the good news'" (Mark 1:14–15). This call to conversion announces the solemn opening of Lent. Participants are marked with ashes, and the words, "Repent, and believe in the good news," are prayed. This blessing is understood as a personal acceptance of the desire to take on the life of penance for the sake of the gospel.

The example of Jesus in the desert for forty days—a time

during which he fasted and prayed—is imitated. It is time to center attention on conversion. During Lent, the expectation is to examine our lives and, through the practice of prayer, fasting, and works of charity, seek to conform our lives to Christ's. For some, this conversion will be a turning from sin to grace. For others, it will be a gracious turning toward the mystery of God in Christ. Whatever the pattern chosen by a particular pilgrim for an observance of Lent, it is hoped that this book will provide a useful support in the effort.

PART I

~~~~~~

READINGS *for* LENT

DAY 1

Ash Wednesday

A PROMISE FOR LENT

I have slowly become aware of what my Lenten practice might be. It might be the development of some type of "holy indifference" toward the many small rejections I am subject to, and a growing attachment to the Lord and his passion.

I am constantly surprised at how hard it is for me to deal with the little rejections people inflict on each other day by day....This atmosphere often leaves me with a feeling of being rejected and left alone. When I swallow these rejections, I get quickly depressed and lonely; then I am in danger of becoming resentful....

But maybe all of this is the other side of a deep mystery, the mystery that we have no lasting dwelling place on this earth and that only God loves us the way we desire to be loved. Maybe all these small rejections are reminders that I am a traveler on the way to a sacred place where God holds me in the palm of his hand.

HENRI J. M. NOUWEN, *¡GRACIAS! A LATIN AMERICAN JOURNAL*

A PLAN FOR LIFE

"Revere the Lord all your days...and refuse to sin or to transgress his commandments. Live uprightly all the days of your life, and do not walk in the ways of wrongdoing; for those who act in accordance with truth will prosper in all their activities. To all those who practice righteousness give alms from your possessions, and do not let your eye begrudge the gift when you make it. Do not turn your face away from anyone who is poor, and the face of God will not be turned away from you. If you have many possessions, make your gift from them in proportion; if few, do not be afraid to give according to the little you have. So you will be laying up a good treasure for yourself against the day of necessity. For almsgiving delivers from death and keeps you from going into the Darkness."

TOBIT 4:5–11

PRAYER

Lord, our Savior, let me heed the example of total giving that you demonstrated when you died on the cross for my sins. I pray that my pale imitation of your sacrifice during this Lent may be counted on my behalf "against the day of necessity."

LENTEN ACTION

Just for today, lay up a "good treasure" for yourself by ignoring your selfish wants and needs and choosing instead to seek and do our Lord's will, both at home and at work. Let your rule of thumb be placing the good of others above your own.

Thursday After Ash Wednesday

DISCIPLINE: PREPARING A PLACE FOR GOD

*D*iscipline in the spiritual life is the concentrated effort to create the space and time where God can become our master and where we can respond freely to God's guidance. Thus, discipline is the creation of boundaries that keep time and space open for God—a time and a place where God's gracious presence can be acknowledged and responded to.

HENRI J. M. NOUWEN, *BREAD FOR THE JOURNEY:*
A DAYBOOK OF WISDOM AND FAITH

THE FRUITS OF DISCIPLINE

> *The one who sees God will accept his discipline,*
> *and those who rise early to seek him will find favor.*
> *The one who seeks the law will be filled with it,*
> *but the hypocrite will stumble at it.*

Those who fear the Lord will form true judgments,
and they will kindle righteous deeds like a light.
The sinner will shun reproof,
and will find a decision according to his liking....

Do not go on a path full of hazards,
and do not stumble at an obstacle twice.
Do not be overconfident on a smooth road,
and give good heed to your paths.
Guard yourself in every act,
for this is the keeping of the commandments.

SIRACH 32:14–17, 20–23

PRAYER

Holy God, give me the discipline it takes to keep my heart open to your word. Do not let the anger of resentment sidetrack me from the priority of seeking my true home with you. Please give me what it takes to recognize that any personal rejections, real or imagined, are only reminders of an imperfect world. Bestow your grace on me so that life's disappointments will bring out the best in me and not the worst. Amen.

LENTEN ACTION

Make it a point to retreat from life's fast lane for the duration of this Lenten observance in order to nurture and grow an attachment to the Lord's incarnation, passion, death, and resurrection. Select and set aside a prayer time to meditate and respond to God's gracious presence.

DAY 3

Friday After Ash Wednesday

PREOCCUPATIONS

We modern Westerners are so busy with ourselves, so preoccupied with the question of whether we do justice to our own selves, that the experience of the "transcendent" becomes practically impossible....In this way of thinking there is scarcely room for Him who speaks whenever we are silent and who comes in whenever we have emptied ourselves. Instead of making ourselves susceptible to the experience of the transcendent God, we, busy with many things, begin to seek after the small flighty sensations brought about by the artificial stimulation of the senses.

HENRI J. M. NOUWEN,
THOMAS MERTON: CONTEMPLATIVE CRITIC

WISDOM AND JOY

My brothers and sisters, whenever you face trials of any kind, consider it nothing but joy, because you know that the testing of your faith produces endurance; and let endurance have its full effect, so that you may be mature and complete, lacking in nothing....

Let the believer who is lowly boast in being raised up, and the rich in being brought low, because the rich will disappear like a flower in the field. For the sun rises with its scorching heat and withers the field; its flower falls, and its beauty perishes. It is the same way with the rich; in the midst of a busy life, they will wither away.

JAMES 1:2–4, 9–11

PRAYER

Almighty God, help me joyfully to put "first things first" today. Forgive me when I have allowed the artificial concerns of this whirlwind life to overwhelm the space in my heart that should be prepared for your presence. When I become preoccupied with self, put me back on the track of commitment to you. Amen.

LENTEN ACTION

Give your energy today to holding yourself accountable for your actions. Promise yourself to give up just one self-indulgence for the day; for example, a morning cup of caffeine, the daily newspaper, dessert after dinner, or so on.

DAY 4

Saturday After Ash Wednesday

A Time to Reconcile and Refocus

I am certainly not ready for Lent yet....I could have used a few more weeks to get ready for this season of repentance, prayer, and preparation....

I spoke about how Jesus stressed the hidden life. Whether we give alms, prayer, or fast, we are to do it in a hidden way, not to be praised by people but to enter into closer communion with God. Lent is a time of returning to God. It is a time to confess how we keep looking for joy, peace, and satisfaction in many people and things surrounding us, without really finding what we desire. Only God can give us what we want....Lent is a time of refocusing, of reentering the place of truth, of reclaiming our true identity.

HENRI J. M. NOUWEN, SABBATICAL JOURNEY:
THE DIARY OF HIS FINAL YEAR

> *You have forgotten the LORD, your Maker,*
> > *who stretched out the heavens*
> > *and laid the foundations of the earth.*
> *You fear continually all day long*
> > *because of the fury of the oppressor,*
> *who is bent on destruction.*
> > *But where is the fury of the oppressor?*
> *The oppressed shall speedily be released;*
> > *they shall not die and go down to the Pit,*
> > *nor shall they lack bread.*
> *For I am the LORD your God,*
> > *who stirs up the sea so that its waves roar—*
> > *The LORD of hosts is his name.*
> *I have put my words in your mouth,*
> > *and hidden you in the shadow of my hand.*

ISAIAH 51:13–16

PRAYER

Savior God, teach me how to reconcile and resolve my internal warfare, confusion, and dissent, so that I can find the calm and hidden place where your peace and protection reside. Let this calm within be the basis for my reconciliation with others. And help me to neutralize the temptations and easy enticements of modern life. Amen.

LENTEN ACTION

Look closely at one difficulty you perceive in your life. Give up being the "victim" in this situation and plan to take one positive step to resolve this issue and move toward a settlement. Ask for God's help in this process.

First Sunday in Lent

THE GIFT OF FRIENDSHIP

*T*here is a twilight zone in our own hearts that we ourselves cannot see. Even when we know quite a lot about ourselves—our gifts and weaknesses, our ambitions and aspirations, our motives and drives—large parts of ourselves remain in the shadow of consciousness.

This is a very good thing. We will always remain partially hidden to ourselves. Other people, especially those who love us, can often see our twilight zones better than we ourselves can. The way we are seen and understood by others is different from the way we see and understand ourselves.

HENRI J. M. NOUWEN, *BREAD FOR THE JOURNEY:*
A DAYBOOK OF WISDOM AND FAITH

THE VALUE OF FRIENDSHIP

Two are better than one, because they have a good reward for their toil. For if they fall, one will lift up the other; but woe to one who is alone and falls and does not have another to help. Again, if two lie together, they keep warm, but how can one keep warm alone? And though one might prevail against another, two will withstand one. A threefold cord is not quickly broken.

ECCLESIASTES 4:9–12

PRAYER

Loving God, take my poor offering of friendship and remind me every day of your invitation to journey with you to the Easter miracle of the Resurrection. Allow me to accept the weaknesses and defects that you and others see in me, but which are hidden from me. Lift me up when I fall and always let me reach, not reject, your outstretched hand of welcome and forgiveness. And, keep my sins and doubts from leaching the joy out of life. Amen.

LENTEN ACTION

Mentally bless each person you meet today and salute them with loving cheerfulness. Be quick to applaud the accomplishments of others just as our Lord applauds yours.

DAY 6

Monday of the First Week of Lent

HEART OF COURAGE

The word courage comes from *coeur*, which means "heart." To have courage is to listen to our heart, to speak from our heart, and to act from our heart....Often we debate current issues and express our opinions about them. But courage is taking a stance, even an unpopular stance, not because we think differently from others but because from the center of our being we realize how to respond to the situation we are in. Courage does not require spectacular gestures. Courage often starts in small corners: it is courageous not to participate in gossip, not to talk behind someone's back, not to ridicule another. It is courageous to think well of other people and be grateful to them....It is courageous to reach out to a poor person, to spend time with a troubled child, to participate in action to prevent war and violence.

HENRI J. M. NOUWEN,
SABBATICAL JOURNEY: THE DIARY OF HIS FINAL YEAR

COURAGE OF CONVICTION

[Jesus'] disciples said, "Yes, now you are speaking plainly, not in any figure of speech! Now we know that you know all things, and do not need to have anyone question you; by this we believe that you came from God." Jesus answered them, "Do you now believe? The hour is coming, indeed it has come, when you will be scattered, each one to his home, and you will leave me alone. Yet I am not alone because the Father is with me. I have said this to you, so that you may have peace. In the world you face persecution. But take courage; I have conquered the world!"

JOHN 16:29–33

PRAYER

Cherished God, give me true and heartfelt courage that brings strength, resilience, and determination to do what is right rather than what is expedient and convenient. Let my courage be seen in small ways that reflect the essence of your commandments: let me forego gossip and sarcasm, exercise caution with placing blame, refuse to duck away from responsibility, speak wisely at the appropriate moment, and cultivate compassion and understanding. Let me be among those who have the courage of his or her convictions. Amen.

LENTEN ACTION

Choose a new tradition to observe this Lent; for example, decorate your home with reminders of the season (purple, incense, thorny branches), make a cross to adorn a home altar, or, imitating a Greek custom, place six feathers in a potato and remove one during each of the weeks of Lent.

Tuesday of the First Week of Lent

ABANDONMENT TO GOD'S WILL

*T*his morning during my hour of prayer, I tried to come to some level of abandonment to my heavenly Father. It was a hard struggle since so much in me wants to do my will, realize my plans, organize my future, and make my decisions. Still, I know that true joy comes from letting God love me the way God wants, whether it is through illness or health, failure or success, poverty or wealth, rejection or praise. It is hard for me to say, "I shall gratefully accept everything, Lord, that pleases you. Let your will be done." But I know that when I truly believe my Father is pure love, it will become increasingly possible to say these words from the heart.

HENRI J. M. NOUWEN,
THE ROAD TO DAYBREAK: A SPIRITUAL JOURNEY

ABIDE IN GOD'S WILL

Beloved,...Do not love the world or the things in the world. The love of the Father is not in those who love the world; for all that is in the world—the desire of the flesh, the desire of the eyes, the pride in riches—comes not from the Father but from the world. And the world and its desire are passing away, but those who do the will of God live forever.

1 JOHN 2:7, 15–17

PRAYER

Henri Nouwen often said this prayer written by Charles de Foucauld:

I abandon myself into your hands;
    do with me what you will.
Whatever you may do, I thank you;
    I am ready for all, I accept all.
Let only your will be done in me
    and in all your creatures.
    I wish no more than this, O Lord.
Into your hands I commend my soul;
    I offer it to you with all the love of my heart,
    for I love you, Lord,
    and so need to give myself into your hands,
    without reserve and with boundless confidence.
For you are my Father. Amen.

LENTEN ACTION

Instead of refusing to accept God's will, especially when it is harsh, say, "Thy will be done!" Give yourself over to unbounded acceptance of the plan that has been mapped out for you by God.

Wednesday of the First Week of Lent

FORGIVENESS

*T*o forgive another person from the heart is an act of liberation. We set that person free from the negative bonds that exist between us. We say, "I no longer hold your offense against you."... We also free ourselves from the burden of being the "offended one." As long as we do not forgive those who have wounded us, we carry them with us or, worse, pull them as a heavy load. The great temptation is to cling in anger to our enemies and then define ourselves as being offended and wounded by them. Forgiveness, therefore, liberates not only the other but also ourselves.

HENRI J. M. NOUWEN, BREAD FOR THE JOURNEY:
A DAYBOOK OF WISDOM AND FAITH

RECIPROCITY

Jesus said: "If you do good to those who do good to you, what credit is that to you? For even sinners do the same. If you lend to those from whom you hope to receive, what credit is that to you? Even sinners lend to sinners, to receive as much again. But love your enemies, do good, and lend, expecting nothing in return. Your reward will be great, and you will be children of the Most High....

"Do not judge, and you will not be judged; do not condemn, and you will not be condemned. Forgive, and you will be forgiven; give, and it will be given to you."

LUKE 6:33–37

PRAYER

God, my divine advocate, grant me the spirit of authentic forgiveness. Elevate my thoughts from the pit of retribution and negativity to the liberated place where I am free from the bonds of wounded anger. Let you who forgave your executioners inspire me to forego my obsessive victimhood and free my heart to follow your will. Amen.

LENTEN ACTION

Choose one bit of emotional garbage that you are clinging to, get rid of it, and get on with your life. In honor of this act, give a gift to someone else who needs a helping hand.

DAY 9

Thursday of the First Week of Lent

SELF-TRANSFORMATION

*J*esus...told people not to be guided by the behavior of the scribes and Pharisees. Jesus came among us as an equal, a brother....

You will not be able to meet Jesus in your body while your body remains full of doubts and fears. Jesus came to free you from those bonds and so create in you a space where you can be with him....

Do not despair, thinking that you cannot change yourself after so many years. Simply enter into the presence of Jesus as you are and ask him to give you a fearless heart where he can be with you. You cannot make yourself different. Jesus came to give you a new heart, a new spirit, a new mind, and a new body. Let him transform you by his love....

HENRI J. M. NOUWEN, THE INNER VOICE OF LOVE:
A JOURNEY THROUGH ANGUISH TO FREEDOM

CONFORMATION

We know all things work together for good for those who love God, who are called according to his purpose. For those whom he foreknew he also predestined to be conformed to the image of his Son, in order that he might be the firstborn within a large family. And those whom he predestined he also called; and those whom he called he also justified; and those whom he justified he also glorified.

What then are we to say about these things? If God is for us, who is against us? He who did not withhold his own Son, but gave him up for all of us, will he not with him also give us everything else?

ROMANS 8:28–32

PRAYER

Creator God, let me recognize in myself the pride and false piety of one who will not admit of the imperfections of being human. Temper my doubts and fears, restore my commitment to your ways. Keep before me your promise of a new heart and a new spirit; prompt me along the path to this transformation in love and conformation to your image. Amen.

LENTEN ACTION

This Lent keep in mind Martin Buber's observation that "God dwells wherever humans let him in." Take time today to be alone and be aware of the movement of the Holy Spirit within you.

DAY 10

Friday of the First Week of Lent

A CALL TO INTIMACY

*J*esus describes the intimacy that he offers as the connectedness between the vine and its branches. I long to be grafted onto Jesus as a branch onto the vine so that all my life comes from the vine. In communion with Jesus, the vine, my little life can grow and bear fruit. I know it, but I do not live it. Somehow I keep living as if there are other sources of life that I must explore, outside of Jesus. But Jesus keeps saying, "Come back to me, give me all your burdens, all your worries, fears, and anxieties. Trust that with me you will find rest."

HENRI J. M. NOUWEN, *SABBATICAL JOURNEY:*
THE DIARY OF HIS FINAL YEAR

WE ARE THE BRANCHES

Jesus said: "I am the true vine, and my Father is the vine-grower. He removes every branch in me that bears no fruit. Every branch that bears fruit he prunes to make it bear more fruit. You have already been cleansed by the word that I have spoken to you. Abide in me as I abide in you. Just as the branch cannot bear fruit by itself unless it abides in the vine, neither can you unless you abide in me. I am the vine, you are the branches. Those who abide in me and I in them bear much fruit, because apart from me you can do nothing."

JOHN 15:1–5

PRAYER

Generous God, pruner and harvester of all my human efforts, teach me how to celebrate life's pains and sorrows so that I can discover in them a deeper love of you and a stronger hope in your promises. Let me not see loss and failure as setbacks, but as opportunities for a more fruitful life. May you always abide in me. Amen.

LENTEN ACTION

Review a past sorrow and find in it one positive outcome. Discipline yourself to show gratitude throughout this day on at least several occasions. Look even in the smallest corners for opportunities to nurture a thankful heart.

Saturday of the First Week of Lent

TRUST

*D*ying is trusting in the catcher [part of a troupe of trapeze artists]. To care for the dying is to say, "Don't be afraid." Remember that you are the beloved child of God. He will be there when you make your long jump. Don't try to grab him; he will grab you. Just stretch out your arms and hands and trust, trust, trust.

HENRI J. M. NOUWEN, *OUR GREATEST GIFT:*
A MEDITATION ON DYING AND CARING

TREE OF TRUST

Thus says the LORD:
Cursed are those who trust in mere mortals
and make mere flesh their strength,
whose hearts turn away from the LORD.

They shall be like a shrub in the desert,
    and shall not see when relief comes.
They shall live in the parched places of
        the wilderness,
    in an uninhabited salt land.

Blessed are those who trust in the LORD,
    whose trust is the LORD.
They shall be like a tree planted by water,
    sending out its roots by the stream.
It shall not fear when heat comes,
    and its leaves shall stay green;
in the year of drought it is not anxious,
    and it does not cease to bear fruit.

JEREMIAH 17:5–8

PRAYER

Giving and forgiving God, though I pay lip service to my trust in you, I know that in times of serious travail, I become afraid and grasp at straws instead of your saving grace. Help me to rely on you instead of myself when trouble strikes. Give me trust to hold out my hands and know that you are there. Amen.

LENTEN ACTION

Make a list of the gifts you take for granted: life, sight, hearing, mobility, opportunity. Keep this list with you to offset the disappointments that threaten to overwhelm your good judgment and undermine your trust in God's plan.

DAY 12

Second Sunday of Lent

BRINGING PAIN HOME

*Y*our pain is deep, and it won't just go away....Your call is to bring that pain home. As long as your wounded part remains foreign to your adult self, your pain will injure you as well as others. Yes, you have to incorporate your pain into your self and let it bear fruit in your heart and the hearts of others.

This is what Jesus means when he asks you to take up your cross. He encourages you to recognize and embrace your unique suffering and to trust that your way to salvation lies therein. Taking up your cross means, first of all, befriending your wounds and letting them reveal to you your own truth.

HENRI J. M. NOUWEN, *THE INNER VOICE OF LOVE:*
A JOURNEY THROUGH ANGUISH TO FREEDOM

TAKE UP YOUR CROSS

[Jesus] said to them, "If any want to become my followers, let them deny themselves and take up their cross and follow me. For those who want to save their life will lose it, and those who lose their life for my sake, and for the sake of the gospel, will save it. For what will it profit them to gain the whole world and forfeit their life? Indeed what can they give in return for their life?

MARK 8:34–37

PRAYER

Eternal God, I thank you and praise you because in Jesus Christ I have the assurances of salvation. Because of Christ's death on the cross and his resurrection, the door is opened to me to share in life everlasting. Help me to take up my crosses and keep my pain "at home," so that my life may be a living sign of your love. Amen.

LENTEN ACTION

Carry out some "giving" actions. Clean out your closets and donate clean and wearable clothing to a charitable organization. Give blood. Do a favor for a neighbor.

DAY 13

Monday of the Second Week of Lent

CELEBRATE

Celebration is only possible through the deep realization that life and death are never found completely separate....Celebration is the acceptance of life in a constantly increasing awareness of its preciousness. And life is precious not only because it can be seen, touched, and tasted, but also because it will be gone one day. When we celebrate a wedding, we celebrate a union as well as a departure, when we celebrate death we celebrate lost friendship as well as gained liberty. There can be tears after weddings and smiles after funerals. We can indeed make our sorrows, just as much as our joys, a part of our celebration of life in the deep realization that life and death are not opponents but do, in fact, kiss each other at every moment of our existence.

HENRI J. M. NOUWEN, *CREATIVE MINISTRY*

A Celebration From Death to Life

[The Prodigal Son] went to his father. But while he was still far off, his father saw him and was filled with compassion; he ran and put his arms around him and kissed him. Then the son said to him, "Father, I have sinned against heaven and before you; I am no longer worthy to be called your son." But the father said to his slaves, "Quickly, bring out a robe—the best one—and put it on him; put a ring on his finger and sandals on his feet. And get the fatted calf and kill it, and let us eat and celebrate; for this son of mine was dead and is alive again; he was lost and is found!" And they began to celebrate.

LUKE 15:20–24

Prayer

Welcoming God, help me to know that my security is in you alone, that life here is not a bowl of cherries but also comes with pits, that it is a mixture of tears and laughter, sorrow and joy, celebration and mourning. Give me the grace to remember that my life is an unearned gift from you, and death is not the finish line but a doorway to a resting place in your loving arms. Amen.

Lenten Action

Plan to become involved this Lent in one parish or community activity that ministers to others. Know that in service to others lies happiness.

DAY 14

Tuesday of the Second Week of Lent

PRACTICE PRUDENCE

*A*s a child of God, you need to be prudent. You cannot simply walk around in this world as if nothing and no one can harm you. You remain extremely vulnerable. The same passions that make you love God may be used by the powers of evil.

The children of God need to support, protect, and hold one another close to God's heart. You belong to a minority in a large, hostile world. As you become more aware of your true identity as a child of God, you will also see more clearly the many forces that try to convince you that all things spiritual are false substitutes for the real things of life.

HENRI J. M. NOUWEN, *THE INNER VOICE OF LOVE:*
A JOURNEY THROUGH ANGUISH TO FREEDOM

THE GIFT OF PRUDENCE

I, wisdom, live with prudence,
*   and I attain knowledge and discretion.*
The fear of the LORD is hatred of evil.
Pride and arrogance and the way of evil
*   and perverted speech I hate.*
I have good advice and sound wisdom;
*   I have insight, I have strength.*
By me kings reign,
*   and rulers decree what is just;*
by me rulers rule,
*   and nobles, all who govern rightly.*

PROVERBS 8:12–16

PRAYER

God of wisdom and love, help me to see that I am your beloved, that your truth is my light in this dark world, and that your steady hand is my joy and my safety net. Grant me the prudence and perception to recognize those deceptive lures that obstruct and pervert my attention and sidetrack my path to you. Help me to learn to count on your infinite skill to guide me clearly in a hostile world. Amen.

LENTEN ACTION

Today practice listening with all your heart and mind. Listen to others. Listen to God.

DAY 15

Wednesday of the Second Week of Lent

SUSTAINMENT

To take the holy scriptures and read them is the first thing we have to do to open ourselves to God's call. Reading the scriptures is not as easy as it seems....We tend to make anything and everything we read subject to analysis and discussion. But the word of God should lead us first of all to contemplation and meditation. Instead of taking the words apart, we should bring them together in our innermost being; instead of wondering if we agree or disagree, we should wonder which words are directly spoken to us and connect directly with our personal story. Instead of thinking about the words as potential subjects for an interesting dialogue..., we should be willing to let them penetrate into the most hidden corners of our hearts, even to those places where no other word has yet found entrance.

HENRI J. M. NOUWEN, *REACHING OUT:*
THE THREE MOVEMENTS OF THE SPIRITUAL LIFE

THE AUTHORITY OF THE WORD

Jesus said to them,… "The Father loves the Son and shows him all that he himself is doing; and he will show him greater works than these, so that you will be astonished. Indeed, just as the Father raises the dead and gives them life, so also the Son gives life to whomever he wishes. The Father judges no one but has given all judgment to the Son, so that all may honor the Son just as they honor the Father. Anyone who does not honor the Son does not honor the Father who sent him. Very truly, I tell you, anyone who hears my word and believes him who sent me has eternal life, and does not come under judgment, but has passed from death to life."

JOHN 5:19–24

PRAYER

Steadfast God, grant me the openness to read and accept the words of your holy Scriptures as truth for my inner being, as a springboard for meditation, as urgent messages directed to the hidden places of my heart. Also grant me the willingness to listen and connect with your teachings. Keep me from stumbling over their simplicity. Amen.

LENTEN ACTION

Choose a passage from holy Scripture that is significant to you and memorize it.

DAY 16

Thursday of the Second Week of Lent

POSITIVE POWERLESSNESS

*G*od became a little baby. Who can be afraid of a little baby?…
That's the mystery of the incarnation. God became human,
in no way different from other human beings, to break through
the walls of power in total weakness. That's the story of Jesus.

And how did that story end? It ended on a cross, where the
same human person hangs naked with nails through his hands
and feet. The powerlessness of the manger has become the powerlessness of the cross….He hangs there, his flesh torn apart by
lead-filled whips, his heart broken by the rejection of his friends
and abuse from his enemies, his mind tortured by anguish, his
spirit shrouded in the darkness of abandonment—total weakness, total powerlessness. That's how God chose to reveal to us
the divine love.

HENRI J. M. NOUWEN, *FINDING MY WAY HOME:*
PATHWAYS TO LIFE AND THE SPIRIT

STRENGTH OF THE LOWLY

Why do you say, O Jacob,
and speak, O Israel,
"My way is hidden from the LORD,
and my right hand is disregarded by my God"?
Have you not known? Have you not heard?
The LORD is the everlasting God,
the Creator of the ends of the earth.
He does not faint or grow weary;
his understanding is unsearchable.
He gives power to the faint,
and strengthens the powerless.
Even youths will faint and be weary,
and the young will fall exhausted;
but those who wait for the LORD shall renew their strength,
they shall mount up with wings like eagles,
they shall run and not be weary....

ISAIAH 40:27–31

PRAYER

Sustainer God, though I very much wish to be in control, let me recognize the strength of Christ's manger and his cross. Transplant in me your humble heart and your heroic surrender so that I may cast out pride and share in the cup of your tears. Amen.

LENTEN ACTION

Promise yourself that you will maintain a dignified silence (just as Jesus did at his trial), at a point where you are eager to contribute your two-cents' worth or when you feel a strong need to defend yourself from criticism.

Friday of the Second Week of Lent

FAITHFULNESS

I now know...that there is a long, hard journey ahead of me. It is the way of living, praying, being with people, caring, eating, drinking, sleeping, reading, and writing in which Jesus is truly the center. I know...that this way exists and that I have not fully found it.

How do I find it? George [Father George Strohmeyer, cofounder of L'Arche community in Pennsylvania] gave me the answer: "Be faithful in your adoration." He did not say, "prayer," or "meditation," or "contemplation." He kept using the word "adoration." This word makes it clear that all the attention must be on Jesus and not on me. To adore is to be drawn away from my own preoccupations into the presence of Jesus. It means letting go of what I want, desire, and have planned and fully trusting in Jesus and his love.

HENRI J. M. NOUWEN, *THE ROAD TO DAYBREAK: A SPIRITUAL JOURNEY*

FAITHFULNESS IN SMALL THINGS

Then Jesus said…"Whoever is faithful in a very little is faithful also in much; and whoever is dishonest in a very little is dishonest also in much. If then you have not been faithful with the dishonest wealth, who will entrust to you the true riches? And if you have not been faithful with what belongs to another, who will give you what is your own? No slave can serve two masters; for a slave will either hate the one and love the other, or be devoted to one and despise the other. You cannot serve God and wealth."

LUKE 16:10–13

PRAYER

God, bread of heaven, let the activities of my daily life be so centered on your presence that my friendship with you is solidly entrenched in my heart of hearts. Let me serve your will and purposes and have the sense to forego the hollow pleasures of success and wealth. Amen.

LENTEN ACTION

Spend a predetermined amount of time in adoration before the Blessed Sacrament. Make a list of the places in your area that have Perpetual Adoration so that you might take the opportunity to visit more frequently. Be faithful in continuing this practice after Lent is over.

DAY 18

Saturday of the Second Week of Lent

ACCEPTANCE

*C*are for your fellowman means a growing acceptance. This acceptance led Jesus and his disciples to where they didn't want to go, to the cross. That is also the road for the [person] who prays. When you are still young and not yet adult, you want to hold everything in your own hands, but if you have your hands open toward prayer, you are able to stretch out your arms and let yourself be led without knowing where. You know only the freedom which God's breath has brought you will lead to new life, even if the cross is the only sign of it you can see.

HENRI J. M. NOUWEN, *WITH OPEN HANDS*

LOVE IS ACCEPTANCE

Jesus said to Simon Peter, "Simon son of John, do you love me more than these?" He said to him, "Yes, Lord; you know that I love you." Jesus said to him, "Feed my lambs." A second time he said to him, "Simon son of John, do you love me?" He said to him, "Yes, Lord; you know that I love you." Jesus said to him, "Tend my sheep." He said to him the third time, "Simon, son of John, do you love me?" Peter felt hurt because he said to him the third time, "Do you love me?" And he said to him, "Lord, you know everything; you know that I love you." Jesus said to him, "Feed my sheep. Very truly, I tell you, when you were younger, you used to fasten your own belt and to go wherever you wished. But when you grow old, you will stretch out your hands, and someone else will fasten a belt around you and take you where you do not wish to go."

JOHN 21:15–18

PRAYER

God of peace, though you have given me my own special cross just as you gave your Son the circumstances of his crucifixion, let me embrace my cross and shoulder it willingly as befits your follower. Though I may not always recognize this cross—which is often cleverly camouflaged—let me accept it as part of your will for me. Even though my cross may be an invisible one, let me see this challenge as a sign of your divine favor. Amen.

LENTEN ACTION

Choose a cross to wear daily during the next days of Lent. Let it be always a sign of solidarity with Jesus rather than a mere decoration.

DAY 19

Third Sunday of Lent

HOPE

A [person] with hope does not get tangled up with concerns for how his wishes will be fulfilled. So, too, his prayer is not directed toward the gift, but toward the one who gives it. His prayer might still contain just as many desires, but ultimately it is not a question of having a wish come true but of expressing an unlimited faith in the giver of all good things....For the prayer of hope it is essential that there are no guarantees asked, no conditions posed, and no proofs demanded, only that you expect everything from the other without binding him. Hope is based on the premise that the other gives only what is good. Hope includes an openness by which you wait for the other to make his loving promise come true, even though you never know when, where or how this might happen.

HENRI J. M. NOUWEN, *WITH OPEN HANDS*

SEIZE THE HOPE

When God desired to show even more clearly to the heirs of the promise the unchangeable character of his purpose, he guaranteed it by an oath, so that through two unchangeable things, in which it is impossible that God would prove false, we who have taken refuge might be strongly encouraged to seize the hope set before us. We have this hope, a sure and steadfast anchor of the soul, a hope that enters the inner shrine behind the curtain, where Jesus, a forerunner on our behalf, has entered.

HEBREWS 6:17–20

PRAYER

Good Shepherd of all, help me to hear your voice of assurance when I am lost and hopeless. Let me find rest and safety in your presence. Though I may be tempted to be full of fear and self-pity, though I may wish to run away from you, please never give up on me. Amen.

LENTEN ACTION

Establish a "prayer place" in your home. Adorn it with images, books, and music that foster prayer and contemplation. Use this spot today and as often as possible in the future.

Monday of the Third Week of Lent

RECEPTIVITY

It is difficult to confess that perhaps the greatest service we can offer to our fellow [human beings] is to receive and allow *them* the happiness of giving. For much of the happiness in our lives is derived from the fact that we can give and though our friends have been willing to receive our gifts, to make them part of their lives, and to allow themselves to become dependent on us through them. We feel happy when we see the picture we gave our friends displayed most advantageously on a wall of the living room. The question is: Would we have given [our friend] the freedom to put it in the attic?...

As long as we keep living with the wrong supposition that giving is our first task, our scotosis [darkness] cannot be healed, and the most creative insights will stay out of our consciousness.

HENRI J. M. NOUWEN, *CREATIVE MINISTRY*

RECEIVE THE JOY OF THE LORD

I, Ezra, received a command from the Lord on Mount Horeb to go to Israel. When I came to them they rejected me and refused the Lord's commandment. Therefore I say to you, O nations that hear and understand, "Wait for your shepherd; he will give you everlasting rest, because he who will come at the end of the age is close at hand. Be ready for the rewards of the kingdom, because perpetual light will shine on you forevermore. Flee from the shadow of this age, receive the joy of your glory. I publicly call on my savior to witness. Receive what the Lord has entrusted to you and be joyful, giving thanks to him who has called you to the celestial kingdoms."

2 ESDRAS 2:33–37

PRAYER

Divine Giver, your generosity is so immense. I see your gifts in the smallest of living things and in the grandest sights of mountains, skies, forests, and seas. In this vast panoply, I am so small, and my offerings are so puny. Yet as I respect and give thanks for your works, let me also be grateful for the gifts given to me by my companions here in this life. Grant me the wisdom to accept these gifts with a pure heart. Amen.

LENTEN ACTION

List the gifts that have been given to you that you have overlooked or minimized. Write a prayer of thanksgiving for all these blessings. Nurture your sincere appreciation and concentrate on grateful receiving.

DAY 21

Tuesday of the Third Week of Lent

PREPARE

*L*ife is a long journey of preparation—of preparing oneself to truly die for others. It is a series of little deaths in which we are asked to release many forms of clinging and to move increasingly from needing others to living for them. The many passages we have to make as we grow from childhood to adolescence, from adolescence to adulthood, and from adulthood to old age offer ever-new opportunities to choose for ourselves or to choose for others. During these passages, questions such as: Do I desire power or service; do I want to be visible or remain hidden; do I strive for a successful career or do I keep following my vocation? keep coming up and confront us with hard choices. In this sense, we can speak about life as a long process of dying to self, so that we will be able to live in the joy of God.

HENRI J. M. NOUWEN, *BEYOND THE MIRROR:*
REFLECTIONS ON DEATH AND LIFE

PREPARE FOR THE ONE WHO COMES

The Lord said: "Blessed is that slave whom his master will find at work when he arrives. Truly I tell you, he will put that one in charge of all his possessions. But if that slave says to himself, 'My master is delayed in coming,' and if he begins to beat the other slaves, men and women, and to eat and drink and get drunk, the master of that slave will come on a day when he does not expect him and at an hour that he does not know, and will cut him in pieces, and put him with the unfaithful. That slave who knew what his master wanted, but did not prepare himself or do what was wanted, will receive a severe beating. But the one who did not know and did what deserved a beating will receive a light beating. From everyone to whom much has been given, much will be required; and from the one to whom much has been entrusted, even more will be demanded.

LUKE 12:42–48

PRAYER

God, eternal Father, as I walk my way through this life, I recall that I too easily do what is wrong instead of what is right. But you love me regardless of my sins and infidelities. As I struggle on this path, remind me to choose service over power, a true vocation to your Word rather than a successful career, the anonymity of hidden help to others rather than self aggrandizement. Help me to detach from self so that I may find a true sense of reality. Amen.

LENTEN ACTION

Make an examination of conscience and choose one area to work on and improve with God's help.

DAY 22

Wednesday of the Third Week of Lent

SEEK YOUR TRUE HOME

*O*ne emotion was very strong—that was homecoming. Jesus opened his home to me and seemed to say, "Here is where you belong." The words he spoke to his disciples, "In my Father's house there are many places to live in....I am going now to prepare a place for you" (John 14:2), became very real. The risen Jesus, who now dwells with his Father, was welcoming me home after a long journey.

This experience was the realization of my oldest and deepest desires. Since the first moment of consciousness, I have had to desire to be with Jesus. Now I felt his presence in a most tangible way, as if my whole life had come together and I was being enfolded in love. The homecoming had a real quality of return, a return to the womb of God.

HENRI J. M. NOUWEN,
BEYOND THE MIRROR: REFLECTIONS ON DEATH AND LIFE

JESUS THE HEART OF OUR EXISTENCE

O LORD, you have searched me and known me.
You know when I sit down and when I rise up;
You discern my thoughts from far away.
You search out my path and my lying down,
and are acquainted with all my ways.
Even before a word is on my tongue,
O LORD, you know it completely....

For it was you who formed my inward parts;
you knit me together in my mother's womb.
I praise you, for I am fearfully and wonderfully made....
Your eyes behold my unformed substance.
In your book were written
all the days that were formed for me,
when none of them as yet existed.

PSALM 139:1–4, 13–16

PRAYER

Indwelling God, you know the truth of me even before I was formed in my mother's womb, you know my thoughts even before I apprehend them, you welcome me home into the warmth of your love even when I do not realize that I am lost. I know myself so little even as you know me so well. I cannot fathom the future, but grant me the grace to appreciate the present in that place where I most belong—in your heart. Amen.

LENTEN ACTION

Practice "letting go" of one aspect of the future which is not in your hands. Spend this day in mindfulness of each present moment rather than letting your thoughts and plans race ahead of yourself.

Thursday of the Third Week of Lent

SEEK CONVERSION

*J*esus challenges us to move in a totally new direction. He asks for conversion—that is to say, a complete interior turnaround, a transformation....Everything within us seems set against this way. And yet—every time we take a few steps along it, we become aware that something new is happening within us and experience a desire to try yet another step forward. And so, step by step, we come closer to the heart of God, which is the heart of an undiscriminating, always-forgiving, inexhaustible love.

HENRI J. M. NOUWEN, *LETTERS TO MARC ABOUT JESUS*

THE JOURNEY IS HAZARDOUS

When Jesus saw the crowds, he went up the mountain; and after he sat down, his disciples came to him. Then he began to speak, and taught them, saying...

"Enter through the narrow gate; for the gate is wide and the road is easy that leads to destruction, and there are many who take it. For the gate is narrow and the road is hard that leads to life, and there are few who find it....

"Not everyone who says to me, 'Lord, Lord,' will enter the kingdom of heaven, but only the one who does the will of my Father in heaven. On that day many will say to me, 'Lord, Lord, did we not prophesy in your name, and cast out demons in your name, and do many deeds of power in your name?' Then I will declare to them, 'I never knew you; go away from me, you evildoers.'"

MATTHEW 5:1–2; 7:13–14, 21–23

PRAYER

God of the Narrow Gate, I am often a creature of convenience— convenience foods, convenient access to roads, convenient TV remote controls, convenient drive-up windows, and convenience stores. I know that these and many other aspects of modern life make it easier for me. Even still, I want things and people to change and adapt for my benefit. Help me to remember that the hard and steep way is the path to your house and that I must practice "give and take" rather than the "take and take" of a world revolving around my needs, and wants, my pleasures, my way. Amen.

LENTEN ACTION

Make a list of life's conveniences and "fast" from one or several of them for a day (watching TV without using the remote control or walking up the steps instead of taking the elevator).

DAY 24

Friday of the Third Week of Lent

ACKNOWLEDGE GOD'S LOVE

The most important thing you can say about God's love is that God loves us not because of anything we've done to earn that love, but because God, in total freedom, has decided to love us. At first sight, this doesn't seem to be very inspiring; but if you reflect on it more deeply this thought can affect and influence your life greatly. We're inclined to see our whole existence in terms of quid pro quo. We assume that people will be nice to us if we are nice to them; that they will help us if we help them;...that they will love us if we love them. And so the conviction is deeply rooted in us that being loved is something you have to earn....We can scarcely conceive of getting something for nothing.

HENRI J. M. NOUWEN, *LETTERS TO MARC ABOUT JESUS*

LOVE EVEN YOUR ENEMIES

[Jesus] looked up at his disciples and said: "But I say to you that listen, Love your enemies, do good to those who hate you, bless those who curse you, pray for those who abuse you. If anyone strikes you on the cheek, offer the other also; and from anyone who takes away your coat do not withhold even your shirt. Give to everyone who begs from you; and if anyone takes away your goods, do not ask for them again. Do to others as you would have them do to you."

LUKE 6:27–31

PRAYER

God most high, please take me back again into your love that I can never earn. I confess that I have failed, and that your forgiveness is wholly undeserved. I am mired in the human belief that love is something I earn, that others will only love me if I act as if I love them. What can I do with a love that is not rationed, that is boundless, that cannot be withdrawn. I am truly awed. Grant me the grace to accept this gift. Amen.

LENTEN ACTION

Today pray for any who have abused you, pray for your enemies, and return good for evil.

DAY 25

Saturday of the Third Week of Lent

DESCEND IN IMITATION OF JESUS

*J*esus presents to us the great mystery of the descending way. It is the way of suffering, but also the way to healing. It is the way of humiliation, but also the way to resurrection. It is the way of tears, but of tears that turn into tears of joy....

The descending way of love, the way to the poor, the broken, and oppressed becomes the ascending way of love, the way to joy, peace, and new life. The cross is transformed from a sign of defeat into a sign of victory, from a sign of despair into a sign of hope, from a sign of death into a sign of life....

Each one of us has to seek out his or her own descending way of love....The descending way is a way that is concealed in each person's heart. But because it is so seldom walked on, it is often overgrown with weeds. Slowly but surely we have to clear the weeds, open the way, and set out on it unafraid.

HENRI J. M. NOUWEN, *LETTERS TO MARC ABOUT JESUS*

CLOTHE YOURSELF WITH HUMILITY

Beloved…I exhort the elders among you to tend the flock of God that is in your charge, exercising the oversight, not under compulsion but willingly, as God would have you do it—not for sordid gain but eagerly. Do not lord it over those in your charge, but be examples to the flock. And when the chief shepherd appears, you will win the crown of glory that never fades away….And all of you must clothe yourselves with humility in your dealings with one another, for / "God opposes the proud, / but gives grace to the humble."

1 PETER 4:12; 5:1–5

PRAYER

God of many mercies, help me find the way of descent—the way of humility, of tears, of suffering, of hiddenness. I am often the one who wants to be the "center of attention," the "star of the show," the "leader of the band," the "first in line." In a world that values winning above all, I have trouble knowing that you changed the rules, that as the cross is transformed from a sign of death into an emblem of life, I must seek the lowly path in order to reach the heights of eternal happiness. Keep your light before me always. Amen.

LENTEN ACTION

Give up the upper hand today. Let someone ahead of you in the checkout line, give someone else the right of way in traffic, give credit to someone else.

DAY 26

Fourth Sunday of Lent

OVERCOME FEAR

*N*icodemus admired Jesus but was afraid to lose the respect of his own colleagues. I am becoming more and more aware of the importance of looking at these fearful sympathizers because that is the group I find myself mostly gravitating toward.

I love Jesus but want to hold on to my own friends even when they do not lead me closer to Jesus. I love Jesus but want to hold on to my own independence even when that independence brings me no real freedom....I love Jesus but do not want to give up my writing plans, travel plans, and speaking plans, even when these plans are often more to my glory than to the glory of God.

So I am like Nicodemus, who came by night, said safe things about Jesus to his colleagues, and expressed his guilt by bringing to the grave more myrrh and aloes (John 19:39) than needed or desired.

HENRI J. M. NOUWEN, *THE ROAD TO DAYBREAK: A SPIRITUAL JOURNEY*

OVERCOME TIMIDITY

The crowd said, "This is really the prophet." Others said, "This is the Messiah." But some asked, "Surely the Messiah does not come from Galilee, does he? Has not the scripture said that the Messiah is descended from David and comes from Bethlehem, the village where David lived." So there was a division in the crowd because of [Jesus]....

Then the temple police [who had been ordered to arrest Jesus] went back to the chief priests and Pharisees, who asked them, "Why did you not arrest him?" The police answered, "Never has anyone spoken like this!" Then the Pharisees replied, "Surely you have not been deceived too, have you?...Nicodemus, who had gone to Jesus before, and who was one of them [a Pharisee], asked, "Our law does not judge people without first giving them a hearing to find out what they are doing, does it?" They replied, "Surely you are not also from Galilee, are you? Search and you will see that no prophet is to arise from Galilee."

JOHN 7:40–52

PRAYER

Dearest God, help me to evaluate my motivations and actions in the light of your purposes and not be held sway by the advice of friends and opinion makers. Let me look to you rather than to others for guidance, for in setting that priority I learn to renounce my own will and keep peace with you. Amen.

LENTEN ACTION

Make a list of those things and people who most influence you, for example, friends, family, media, public opinion, and so on. Weed out one of those influences that are most unhealthy. In addition, this Lent make it a point to stand up for one unpopular but morally sound point of view.

DAY 27

Monday of the Fourth Week of Lent

CLAIM YOUR BLESSINGS

*M*y second suggestion for claiming your blessedness is the cultivation of presence. By presence I mean attentiveness to the blessings that come to you day after day, year after year. The problem of modern living is that we are too busy...to notice that we are being blessed. Often, people say good things about us, but we brush them aside with remarks such as, "Oh, don't mention it." These remarks may seem to be expressions of humility, but they are, in fact, signs that we are not truly present to receive the blessings that are given. It is not easy for us, busy people, to receive a blessing...to stop, listen, pay attention and receive gracefully what is offered to us.

HENRI J. M. NOUWEN, *LIFE OF THE BELOVED: SPIRITUAL LIVING IN A SECULAR WORLD*

FAITH IN HIS PRESENCE

Friends, I know that you acted in ignorance, as did also your rulers. In this way God fulfilled what he had foretold through all the prophets, that his Messiah would suffer. Repent therefore, and turn to God so that your sins may be wiped out, so that times of refreshing may come from the presence of the Lord, and that he may send the Messiah appointed for you, that is, Jesus, who must remain in heaven until the time of universal restoration that God announced long ago.

ACTS 3:17–21

PRAYER

All-powerful God, help me to recognize your glory in every blessing you have bestowed on me, in all that you have created, and especially in other human beings, no matter what their state or circumstance. When I find myself failing to notice the beauty of a moonlit night, the abundance of harvest fruits and vegetables, the perfection of clouds against a blue sky, slow me down and give me gratitude and reverence for all your gifts. Amen.

LENTEN ACTION

Slow down today and savor every moment God has given you.

DAY 28

Tuesday of the Fourth Week of Lent

LEARN FROM THE MASTER

*J*esus can be called Teacher in the fullest sense of the word precisely because He did not cling to His prerogatives but became one of the many who have to learn. His life makes it clear to us that we do not need weapons, that we do not need to hide ourselves or play competitive games with each other. Only he who is not afraid to show his weaknesses and who allows himself to be touched by the tender hand of the Teacher will be able to be a real student.

HENRI J. M. NOUWEN, *CREATIVE MINISTRY*

"TEACHER, WHAT MUST I DO?"

As [Jesus] was setting out on a journey, a man ran up and knelt before him and asked him, "Good Teacher, what must I do to inherit eternal life?" Jesus said to him, "Why do you call me good? No one is good but God alone. You know the commandments: 'You shall not murder; You shall not commit adultery; You shall not steal; You shall not bear false witness; You shall not defraud; Honor your father and mother.'" He said to him, "Teacher, I have kept all these since my youth." Jesus, looking at him, loved him and said, "You lack one thing; go, sell what you own, and give the money to the poor, and you will have treasure in heaven; then come, follow me."

MARK 10:17–22

PRAYER

Teacher God, touch my heart with understanding so that I may discern your perfect ways and follow them. Many times your challenges seem overwhelming to me, and I slink silently away from them. Develop my capabilities so that I can follow you in spite of the sacrifices that you demand. Give me the grace to become a wise learner, one who is not a fiercely competitive game player but one who can humbly value and follow your truth. Amen.

LENTEN ACTION

Saint Antony, father of the monastic way of living, heard Jesus' words to "sell what you have, give the money to the poor, and come follow me" and did exactly that. He ended up alone in the desert. While we may be more like the young man than Saint Antony, at least make one significant contribution this Lent to aid the poor.

DAY 29

Wednesday of the Fourth Week of Lent

LOOK FOR THE SPIRIT

*T*he spiritual life can only be real when it is lived in the midst of the pains and joys of the here and now. Therefore we need to begin with a careful look at the way we think, speak, feel, and act…in order to become more fully aware of our hunger for the Spirit. As long as we have only a vague inner feeling of discontent with our present way of living, and only an indefinite desire for "things spiritual," our lives will continue to stagnate….

Our first task is to dispel this vague, murky feeling of discontent and to look critically at how we are living our lives. This requires honesty, courage, and trust. We must honestly unmask and courageously confront our many self-deceptive games. We must trust that our honesty and courage will lead us not to despair, but to a new heaven and a new earth.

HENRI J. M. NOUWEN, *MAKING ALL THINGS NEW:*
AN INVITATION TO THE SPIRITUAL LIFE

Do Not Be Sad

[Jesus] began to speak, and taught them, saying: "Do not worry about your life, what you will eat or what you will drink, or about your body, what you will wear. Is not life more than food, and the body more than clothing? Look at the birds of the air; they neither sow nor reap nor gather into barns, and yet your heavenly Father feeds them. Are you not of more value than they? And can any of you by worrying add a single hour to your span of life?...Indeed your heavenly Father knows that you need all these things. But strive first for the kingdom of God and his righteousness, and all these things will be given to you as well."

MATTHEW 6:25–27, 32–33

Prayer

Beloved God, chase away my melancholy and ennui with the gift of your grace. Let me actively pursue your spiritual gifts instead of putting off this pursuit out of a vague sense of boredom and doubt. Give me the honesty to unmask my many self-deceptive games so that I may strive wholeheartedly for the kingdom of God. Amen.

Lenten Action

In honor of our heavenly Father, feed the birds this Lent. Perhaps create festive decorations of seeds and nuts to attract and feed hungry birds and squirrels. Do not forget to put out fresh water.

DAY 30

Thursday of the Fourth Week of Lent

SEE BOREDOM AS A WARNING

*B*oredom is a sentiment of disconnectedness. While we are busy with many things, we wonder if what we do makes any real difference. Life presents itself as a random and unconnected series of activities and events over which we have little or no control. To be bored, therefore, does not mean that we have nothing to do, but that we question the value of the things we are so busy doing. The great paradox of our time is that many of us are busy and bored at the same time....While we can hardly keep up with our many tasks and obligations, we are not so sure that it would make any difference if we did nothing at all.

HENRI J. M. NOUWEN, *MAKING ALL THINGS NEW: AN INVITATION TO THE SPIRITUAL LIFE*

THE BETTER PART

Now as they went on their way, [Jesus] entered a certain village, where a woman named Martha welcomed him into her home. She had a sister named Mary, who sat at the Lord's feet and listened to what he was saying. But Martha was distracted by her many tasks; so she came to him and asked, "Lord, do you not care that my sister has left me to do all the work by myself? Tell her then to help me." But the Lord answered her, "Martha, Martha, you are worried and distracted by many things; there is need of only one thing. Mary has chosen the better part, which will not be taken away from her."

LUKE 10:38–42

PRAYER

Dearest Father, help me to recognize the boredom of a pointlessly busy life filled with disconnects from the grace and energy needed to fulfill your purpose. While Christ has given his life for my salvation, I seem to be lost on the track of an alternate universe that focuses on mindless activities and needless busy work. Let me not be distracted, as was Martha by her many self-imposed tasks, but let me know when it is time just to sit and listen to your voice. Amen.

LENTEN ACTION

Give up an extraneous task this Lent and concentrate instead on finding the "better part." Give up one of the ingrained cultural expectations that are external signs of accomplishment. Give up your sleep-walking in favor of a radical effort for God's cause.

DAY 31

Friday of the Fourth Week of Lent

A CALL TO VOCATION

We seldom realize fully that we are sent to fulfill God-given tasks. We act as if we have to choose how, where, and with whom to live. We act as if we were simply dropped down in creation and have to decide how to entertain ourselves until we die. But we were sent into the world by God, just as Jesus was. Once we start living our lives with that conviction, we will soon know what we were sent to do.

HENRI J. M. NOUWEN, *BREAD FOR THE JOURNEY: A DAYBOOK OF WISDOM AND FAITH*

GOD'S PURPOSE

> *Those who keep the commandment will live;*
> *those who are heedless of their ways will die.*
> *Whoever is kind to the poor lends to the LORD,*
> *and will be repaid in full....*
> *Listen to advice and accept instruction,*
> *that you may gain wisdom for the future.*
> *The human mind may devise many plans,*
> *but it is the purpose of the LORD*
> *that will be established.*

PROVERBS 19:16–21

PRAYER

All-wise God, our Father, I have spent a significant amount of my time on this planet finding my earthly vocation—an effort filled with day planners, multitasking, career striving, and celebrations of human accomplishments. This search is really one of the huffing and puffing of a pride-filled competitor. Let me instead find my true vocation—one that is grounded in you. Remind me frequently that human plans are hollow, but the purposes of the Lord are paramount. Amen.

LENTEN ACTION

Examine your current role in life, your career. Devise one way to bring Christ closer to you in your work environment. Implement this reorientation over the course of the next few weeks.

DAY 32

Saturday of the Fourth Week of Lent

TRUE LISTENING

*I*t is clear that we are usually surrounded by so much inner and outer noise that it is hard to truly hear our God when he is speaking to us. We have often become deaf, unable to know when God calls us and unable to understand in which direction he calls us. Thus our lives have become absurd. In the word *absurd*, we find the Latin word *surdus*, which means "deaf." A spiritual life requires discipline because we need to learn to listen to God, who constantly speaks but whom we seldom hear. When, however, we learn to listen, our lives become obedient lives. The word *obedient* comes from the Latin word *audire*, which means "to listen."

HENRI J. M. NOUWEN, *MAKING ALL THINGS NEW:*
AN INVITATION TO THE SPIRITUAL LIFE

A Still Small Voice

The Lord said to Elijah, "Go out and stand on the mountain before the LORD, for the LORD is about to pass by." Now there was a great wind, so strong that it was splitting mountains and breaking rocks in pieces before the LORD, but the LORD was not in the wind; and after the wind an earthquake, but the LORD was not in the earthquake; and after the earthquake a fire, but the LORD was not in the fire; and after the fire a sound of sheer silence. When Elijah heard it, he wrapped his face in his mantle and went out and stood at the entrance of the cave. Then there came a voice to him that said, "What are you doing here, Elijah?" He answered, "I have been very zealous for the LORD, God of hosts; for the Israelites have forsaken your covenant, thrown down your altars, and killed your prophets with the sword. I alone am left, and they are seeking my life, to take it away."

1 KINGS 19:11–14

PRAYER

Lord, God of all, I strongly believe that you have illumined my soul with the divine life of your grace. Though you have walked by my side, suddenly I feel that your voice has disappeared. I feel alone and abandoned. I seem to be searching for you in all the wrong places. Help me to find your voice again—not in the dramatic events of fire and earthquake—but in the silence of my own soul. Please answer soon, Lord. I am waiting. Amen.

LENTEN ACTION

Take time to write a brief autobiography of your spiritual journey. Include the good and the bad. Record especially those times when God's voice was most clear and those times when you were overcome with deafness to his message.

DAY 33

Fifth Sunday of Lent

LIVE THE PAIN

*T*he great challenge is *living* your wounds through instead of *thinking* them through. It is better to cry than to worry, better to feel your wounds deeply than to understand them, better to let them enter into your silence than to talk about them. The choice you face constantly is whether you are taking your wounds to your head or your heart. In your head you can analyze them, find their causes and consequences, and coin words to speak and write about them. But no final healing is likely to come from that source. You need to let your wounds go down to your heart. Then you can live through them and discover that they will not destroy you.

HENRI J. M. NOUWEN, *THE INNER VOICE OF LOVE:*
A JOURNEY THROUGH ANGUISH TO FREEDOM

ENDURE SUFFERING AS JESUS DID

If you endure [being beaten] when you do right and suffer for it, you have God's approval. For to this you have been called, because Christ also suffered for you, leaving you an example, so that you should follow in his steps.

> *"He committed no sin,*
> *and no deceit was found in his mouth."*

When he was abused, he did not return abuse; when he suffered, he did not threaten; but he entrusted himself to the one who judges justly.

1 PETER 2:20–23

PRAYER

God of wholeness and healing, I know that I am afraid of pain and acutely conscious of being harmed and hurt. Help me avoid my pattern of cause-and-effect, of rationalizing my wounds. Instead, let the soothing oil of your mercy heal my wounds; let me live through the pain and recognize that your joy is truly on the other side. Amen.

LENTEN ACTION

Pick one of the corporal works of mercy to practice over the next few days. The corporal works of mercy are as follows: To feed the hungry, to give drink to the thirsty, to clothe the naked, to visit the imprisoned, to shelter the homeless, to visit the sick, to bury the dead.

DAY 34

Monday of the Fifth Week of Lent

SPEAK GOD'S WORD BOLDLY

*L*et me retain innocence and simplicity in the midst of this complex world. I realize that I have to be informed, that I have to study the many problems facing the world, and that I have to try to understand as well as possible the dynamics of our contemporary society. But what really counts is that all this information, knowledge, and insight allow me to speak more clearly and unambiguously your truthful word. Do not allow evil powers to seduce me with the complexities of the world's problems, but give the strength to think clearly, speak freely, and act boldly in your service.

HENRI J. M. NOUWEN,
A CRY FOR MERCY: PRAYERS FROM THE GENESEE

THE SPIRIT WILL GIVE YOU WORDS

These twelve Jesus sent out with the following instructions:...
"I am sending you out like sheep into the midst of wolves; so
be wise as serpents and innocent as doves. Beware of them,
for they will hand you over to councils and flog you in their
synagogues; and you will be dragged before governors and
kings because of me, as a testimony to them and the Gentiles.
When they hand you over, do not worry about how you are
to speak or what you are to say; for what you are to say will
be given to you at that time; for it is not you who speak, but
the Spirit of your Father speaking through you."

MATTHEW 10:16–20

PRAYER

Holy God, I sometimes lack the courage to live out my
Christian convictions, especially as I confront a world in
which knowledge is often corrupted and information is
twisted to fit the circumstances. All these complexities
can overshadow the Good News of the Gospels and ma-
nipulate this world of ours toward disaster. Grant me the
courage to show the dove of innocence and simplicity in
a world so full of serpents. Give me strength to remain
detached from the world's destructiveness and help me
to proclaim the goodness of God with boldness and assurance. Amen.

LENTEN ACTION

Pray the rosary today, meditating on the sorrowful mys-
teries. If possible, give a rosary to someone as a gift, along
with instructions on how to pray it, if necessary.

DAY 35

Tuesday of the Fifth Week of Lent

BE COMPASSIONATE, NOT COMPETITIVE

This all-pervasive competition, which reaches into the smallest corners of our relationships, prevents us from entering into full solidarity with each other, and stands in the way of our being compassionate. We prefer to keep compassion on the periphery of our competitive lives. Being compassionate would require giving up dividing lines and relinquishing differences and distinctions. And that would mean losing our identities. This makes it clear why the call to be compassionate is so frightening and evokes such deep resistance.

HENRI J. M. NOUWEN, DONALD P. MCNEILL,
AND DOUGLAS A. MORRISON,
COMPASSION: A REFLECTION ON CHRISTIAN LIFE

THE BEST PLACES

James and John, the sons of Zebedee, came forward to [Jesus] and said to him, "Teacher, we want you to do for us whatever we ask of you." And he said to them, "What is it you want me to do for you?" And they said to him, "Grant us to sit, one at your right hand and one at your left, in your glory." But Jesus said to them, "You do not know what you are asking."...

When the ten heard this, they began to be angry with James and John. So Jesus called them and said to them... Whoever wishes to become great among you must be your servant, and whoever wishes to be first among you must be lover of all."

MARK 10:35–38, 41–44

PRAYER

Guardian God, I am often caught up in competitive games—who is better, who is richer, who is nicer, who is more attractive. This competition keeps me separate from others, making me a loner rather than a comrade and a person in solidarity with others. Help me to live a life where distinctions fade away and differences are downplayed, where I become a lover of all rather than a lover of self. Amen.

LENTEN ACTION

Show compassion by choosing to practice one of the spiritual works of mercy. They are as follows: To admonish the sinner, to instruct the ignorant, to counsel the doubtful, to comfort the sorrowful, to bear wrongs patiently, to forgive all injuries, to pray for the living and the dead.

DAY 36

Wednesday of the Fifth Week of Lent

BE CHRISTLIKE

You are Christian only so long as you look forward to a new world, so long as you constantly pose critical questions to the society you live in, so long as you emphasize the need of conversion both for yourself and for the world, so long as you in no way let yourself become established in a situation of seeming calm, so long as you stay unsatisfied with the status quo and keep saying that a new world is yet to come. You are Christian only when you believe that you have a role to play in the realization of this new kingdom, and when you urge everyone you meet with a holy unrest to make haste so that the promise might soon be fulfilled.

HENRI J. M. NOUWEN, *WITH OPEN HANDS*

CALLED TO BE CHRISTIANS

News of this [preaching to the Hellenists of Antioch] came to the ears of the church in Jerusalem, and they sent Barnabas to Antioch. When he came and saw the grace of God, he rejoiced, and he exhorted them all to remain faithful to the Lord with steadfast devotion....And a great many people were brought to the Lord. Then Barnabas went to Tarsus to look for Saul, and when he had found him, he brought him to Antioch. So it was that for an entire year they met with the church and taught a great many people, and it was in Antioch that the disciples were first called "Christians."

ACTS 11:22–26

PRAYER

Giving and forgiving God, I have called myself your disciple but perhaps this title is truly undeserved. I want to live in comfort even though a life of sacrifice is needed for the world's renewal. I too easily turn a blind eye to injustice and put the oppressed and forgotten into the category of "someday." I hide behind the presumed safety of the status quo, even though you have asked that I work for a new kingdom. Even so, I ask your help to be converted from a member of the present secular society to a willing worker for a new order, and new life, and a new truth. Amen.

LENTEN ACTION

In preparation for Easter, plan to celebrate the sacrament of reconciliation.

DAY 37

Thursday of the Fifth Week of Lent

OPEN YOUR HANDS

How do I open my closed hands? Certainly not by violence. Not by a compulsive decision. Perhaps you can find a way to prayer in the words of the angel to the frightened shepherds.... Don't be afraid of him who wants to enter that space where you live, or to let him see what you are clinging to so anxiously. Don't be afraid to show the clammy coin which will buy so little anyway. Don't be afraid to offer your hate, bitterness, disappointment to him who reveals himself as love. Even if you have little to show, don't be afraid to let it be seen. You keep catching yourself wanting to deceive the other by putting on a semblance of beauty, by holding back everything dirty and spoiled, by clearing a little path that looks very proper. But that is compulsive, forced and artificial.

HENRI J. M. NOUWEN, *WITH OPEN HANDS*

Do Not Be Afraid

I turned to see whose voice it was that spoke to me, and on turning I saw seven golden lampstands, and in the midst of the lampstands I saw one like the Son of Man, clothed with a long robe and with a golden sash across his chest....

When I saw him, I fell at his feet as though dead. But he placed his right hand on me, saying, "Do not be afraid; I am the first and the last, and the living one. I was dead, and see, I am alive for ever and ever."

REVELATION 1:12–13, 17–18

Prayer

God of openness and truth, when I make a clenched hand, let me see it as a symbol of violence and anger. Make my hands open as promises of friendship and love. Open my heart as well so that it is transparent and honest. Let me reveal myself in love and let me no longer rely on the pretense of perfection. Instead, let my sins reveal my humanity. Amen.

Lenten Action

Instead of focusing on the faults of others (which may be mirrors of one's own failings), make a humble assessment of your own acts of greed, selfishness, and unkindness. Make amends to those you have hurt.

DAY 38

Friday of the Fifth Week of Lent

MAKE YOUR LIFE A PRAYER

When your life is more and more becoming a prayer, you notice that you are always busy converting yourself and gaining an ever-deeper understanding of your fellow [human beings]. You notice, too, that prayer is the pulse of the world you live in. If you are really praying, you can't help but have critical questions about the great problems the world is grappling with, and you can't get rid of the idea that a conversion is not only necessary for yourself and your neighbor, but for the entire human community. This conversion of the world means a "turning around," a revolution, which can lead to renewal.

HENRI J. M. NOUWEN, *WITH OPEN HANDS*

RENEWAL

Now you must get rid of all such things—anger, wrath, malice, slander, and abusive language from your mouth. Do not lie to one another, seeing that you have stripped off the old self with its practices and have clothed yourselves with the new self, which is being renewed in knowledge according to the image of its creator. In that renewal there is no longer Greek and Jew, circumcised and uncircumcised, barbarian, Scythian, slave and free; but Christ is all and in all!

COLOSSIANS 3:8–11

PRAYER

God forever glorious, grant me the grace to be counted among your chosen ones, those who are beloved by you. Do this for me in spite of my tendency to cling to my old and sinful practices. Help me to turn my life into an ongoing prayer that smooths the way not only for my own transformation but also for the renewal of the whole human community. Amen.

LENTEN ACTION

Find stories of true personal transformation that also spill over into a conversion for others. Perhaps these stories might come from the lives of the saints, from the history of humanitarian efforts, or from personal witness. Record these stories for your own inspiration and add to them periodically.

DAY 39

Saturday of the Fifth Week of Lent

PRAY FOR DEPENDENCY ON GOD

*P*rayer requires that we stand in God's presence with open hands, naked and vulnerable, proclaiming to ourselves and to others that without God we can do nothing. This is difficult in a climate where the predominant counsel is, "Do your best and God will do the rest." When life is divided into "our best" and "God's rest," we have turned prayer into a last resort to be used only when all our own resources are depleted. Then even the Lord has become the victim of our impatience. Discipleship does not mean to use God when we can no longer function ourselves. On the contrary, it means to recognize that we can do nothing at all, but that God can do everything through us.

HENRI J. M. NOUWEN, DONALD P. MACNEILL,
AND DOUGLAS A. MORRISON,
COMPASSION: A REFLECTION ON THE CHRISTIAN LIFE

STAND FIRM IN PRAYER

Rejoice in the Lord always; again I will say, Rejoice. Let your gentleness be known to everyone. The Lord is near. Do not worry about anything, but in everything by prayer and supplication with thanksgiving let your requests be made known to God. And the peace of God, which surpasses all understanding, will guard your hearts and your minds in Christ Jesus.

PHILIPPIANS 4:4–7

PRAYER

Three-personed God, it truly frightens me to recognize that I am totally dependent on you. I know that my life is not my own, though I arrogantly act as if I am in control. On the contrary, it is you who determines my destiny. Ease my worries over my dependency on you, soften my impatience with your plans for me, and help me to acknowledge that you can do all things through me. Amen.

LENTEN ACTION

Place a bowl of water on the dining room table or somewhere else accessible. Before or after meals, or when entering or leaving the premises, each member of the household can dip a hand in the water in memory of his or her baptism in Christ.

DAY 40

Passion Sunday

ERADICATE BLAME

We spend a lot of energy wondering who can be blamed for our own or other people's tragedies—our parents, ourselves, the immigrants, the Jews, the gays, the blacks, the fundamentalists, the Catholics....

But Jesus doesn't allow us to solve our own or other people's problems through blame. The challenge he poses is to discern in the midst of our darkness the light of God. In Jesus' vision everything, even the greatest tragedy, can become an occasion in which God's works can be revealed.

How radically new my life would be if I were willing to move beyond blaming to proclaiming the works of God....All human beings have their tragedies....We seldom have much control over them. But do we choose to live them as occasions to blame, or as occasions to see God at work?

HENRI J. M. NOUWEN, *THE SABBATICAL JOURNEY*

BLINDNESS AND BLAME

As he [Jesus] walked along, he saw a man blind from birth. His disciples asked him, "Rabbi, who sinned, this man or his parents, that he was born blind?" Jesus answered, "Neither this man nor his parents sinned; he was born blind so that God's works might be revealed in him. We must work the works of him who sent me while it is day; night is coming when no one can work. As long as I am in the world, I am the light of the world."

JOHN 9:1–5

PRAYER

My God and my refuge, strip away my habit of blaming—either others or myself—for any big or little tragedies in my life. Challenge me to move beyond the "blame game" and to understand that these misfortunes and setbacks are not under my control. Teach me instead to live through these events and see them as fruitful opportunities for faith and love. Amen.

LENTEN ACTION

Review past episodes of your life when you were determined to blame others for destructive events. Did you finally acknowledge that blaming is a way to avoid seeing God's hand at work in your life? Are you still relying on blame as a "way out" today? If so, in what way? Are there community "scapegoats" who are blamed for disastrous occurrences? How can those whom we set up as scapegoats be exonerated?

You may also want to observe the tradition of eating figs on Palm Sunday and decorating your home with pussy willows. Or you may wish to select and address Easter cards.

DAY 41

Monday of Passion Week

SEEK SOLITUDE

We know that it is important to spend time in solitude. We even start looking forward to this strange period of uselessness. This desire for solitude is often the first sign of prayer, the first indication that the presence of God's Spirit no longer remains unnoticed. As we empty ourselves of our many worries, we come to know not only with our mind but also with our heart that we never were really alone, that God's Spirit was with us all along.... The pains and struggles we encounter in our solitude thus become a way to hope, because our hope is not based on something that will happen after our sufferings are over, but on the real presence of God's healing Spirit in the midst of these sufferings.

HENRI J. M. NOUWEN, *MAKING ALL THINGS NEW: AN INVITATION TO THE SPIRITUAL LIFE*

DWELL IN EMPTINESS

Since we are justified by faith, we have peace with God through our Lord Jesus Christ, through whom we have obtained access to this grace in which we stand; and we boast in our hope of sharing in the glory of God. And not only that, but we also boast in our sufferings, knowing that suffering produces endurance, and endurance produces character, and character produces hope, and hope does not disappoint us, because God's love has been poured into our hearts through the Holy Spirit.

ROMANS 5:1–5

PRAYER

God of glory, I pray that you will help me build that inner solitude, that secret place of peace, apart from the world, apart from life's pain and struggles. Grant me the spiritual strength to wear the outer world as a loose garment, one that can be quickly shed. If my inner life is strong, if it is lived with you, nothing in the world will seriously upset me. As I practice finding this place of silence, let me cherish it as a place to hear your Word and from which to face the world. Amen.

LENTEN ACTION

This day is the time to actively enter into the Passion of Christ. Jesus did not expect his life on earth to go smoothly just because his Father loved him. Just the opposite occurred, out of the Father's great love he sent his only-begotten Son to an ignominious death on the cross for our benefit. Then we must acknowledge that love is not free of pain, hurt, humiliation, and death. Inventory your sins and find true sorrow for the deeds that brought Jesus to this place of crucifixion.

DAY 42

Tuesday of Passion Week

BE AT HOME

*J*esus, in whom the fullness of God dwells, has become our home. By making his home in us he allows us to make our home in him. By entering into the intimacy of our innermost self he offers us the opportunity to enter into his own intimacy with God. By choosing us as *his* preferred dwelling place he invites us to choose him as *our* preferred dwelling place. This is the mystery of the incarnation. It is beautifully expressed during the Eucharist when the priest pours a little water into the wine, saying: "By the mingling of this water and wine may we come to share in the divinity of him who humbled himself to share in our humanity."

HENRI J. M. NOUWEN, *LIFESIGNS:*
INTIMACY, FECUNDITY, AND ECSTASY IN CHRISTIAN PERSPECTIVE

DWELL IN THE LORD

> *The LORD is my shepherd, I shall not want.*
> *He makes me lie down in green pastures;*
> *he leads me beside still waters;*
> *he restores my soul.*
> *He leads me in right paths*
> *for his name's sake....*
>
> *You prepare a table before me*
> *in the presence of my enemies;*
> *you anoint my head with oil;*
> *my cup overflows.*
> *Surely goodness and mercy shall follow me*
> *all the days of my life,*
> *and I shall dwell in the house of the LORD*
> *my whole life long.*

PSALM 23:1–3, 5–6

PRAYER

Everlasting God, you have offered me an intimate place that I can call "home" where I can rest and be healed. Help me accept this true home, where feelings and emotions can be expressed without censorship. Let this home be a place where it is good to be; a house where love is always present. Amen.

LENTEN ACTION

Remember that the fronds waved in joy by those welcoming Jesus into Jerusalem on Palm Sunday become the ashes of death and dust: the source of the marks that are put on our foreheads at the beginning of Lent. Use this day to examine your own feelings about death. During this week in which Christ faced his death, you may wish to examine your own mortality.

DAY 43

Wednesday of Passion Week

REMEMBER GOD EXISTS

*T*o say with all that we have, think, feel, and are, "God exists," is the most world-shattering statement that a human being can make....Because when God exists, all that *is* flows from God. ...However, as soon as I say, "God exists," my existence no longer can remain the center, because the essence of the knowledge of God reveals my own existence as deriving its total being from God's....I no longer let the knowledge of my existence be the center from which I derive, project, deduct, or intuit the existence of God; I suddenly or slowly find my own existence revealed to me in and through the knowledge of God. Then it becomes real for me that I can love myself and my neighbor only because God has loved me first.

HENRI J. M. NOUWEN, *¡GRACIAS!: A LATIN AMERICAN JOURNAL*

FAITH IN GOD'S EXISTENCE

By faith Abel offered to God a more acceptable sacrifice than Cain's. Through this he received approval as righteous, God himself giving approval to his gifts; he died, but through his faith he still speaks. By faith Enoch was taken so that he did not experience death; and "he was not found, because God had taken him." For it was attested before he was taken away that "he had pleased God." And without faith it is impossible to please God, for whoever would approach him must believe that he exists and that he rewards those who seek him.

HEBREWS 11:4–6

PRAYER

Most high God, you who accepted the gifts of Enoch and Abel, accept also my gift of faith offered always and especially during this Holy Week. I believe with my whole being that you exist and have done so from before the beginning of time. Send me a realization of the magnitude of this belief and make this act of faith a life-changing experience. Let my life be rooted in you. Amen.

LENTEN ACTION

Today recite, renew, and meditate on your baptismal vows or the Nicene Creed.

DAY 44

Holy Thursday

CENTRALITY OF THE EUCHARIST

*T*he Lord is at the center of all things and yet in such a quiet, unobtrusive, elusive way. He lives with us, even physically, but not in the same physical way that other elements are present to us. This transcendent physical presence is what characterizes the Eucharist. It is already the other world present in this one. In the celebration of the Eucharist we are given an enclave in our world of space and time. God in Christ is really here, and yet his physical presence is not characterized by the same limitation of space and time that we know....

Contemplative life is a human response to the fundamental fact that the central things in life, although spiritually perceptible, remain invisible in large measure and can very easily be overlooked....The contemplative looks not so much around things but through them into their center. Through their center he discovers the world of spiritual beauty that is more real, has more density, more mass, more energy, and greater intensity than physical matter.

HENRI J. M. NOUWEN, *THE GENESEE DIARY: REPORT FROM A TRAPPIST MONASTERY*

THE LORD'S SUPPER

When the hour came, he [Jesus] took his place at the table, and the apostles with him. He said to them, "I have eagerly desired to eat this Passover with you before I suffer; for I tell you, I will not eat it until it is fulfilled in the kingdom of God." Then he took a cup, and after giving thanks he said, "Take this and divide it among yourselves; for I tell you that from now on I will not drink of the fruit of the vine until the kingdom of God comes." Then he took a loaf of bread, and when he had given thanks, he broke it and gave it to them, saying, "This is my body, which is given for you. Do this in remembrance of me." And he did the same with the cup after supper, saying, "This cup that is poured out for you is the new covenant in my blood."

LUKE 22:14–20

PRAYER

God of all grace, let the Eucharist, the Bread of Life, always remind me of the breaking of Christ's body and the pouring out of his blood for me and the forgiveness of my sins. Let me shed the false demeanor of Judas, let me always remember his kiss of evil, and never fail to acknowledge my part in this betrayal. Amen.

LENTEN ACTION

Plan and celebrate a Seder, or Passover meal, today. Make it an ecumenical observance of reconciliation and unity.

DAY 45

Good Friday

ADMIT OUR BROKENNESS

About a hundred of us walked from the meeting hall to the Dayspring chapel, each carrying a stone to symbolize our burden and our brokenness. We stopped three times to remember how Jesus is condemned to death, Simon of Cyrene is forced to carry the cross when Jesus falls, and Veronica wipes Jesus' face with her towel. Jesus is nailed to the cross.

Michael, Adam's brother, dressed in an alb and with a crown of thorns on his head, is Jesus....We sing and listen to reflections on the passion of Jesus. In the chapel we place our stones on or around the cross....Lorenzo hammers three big nails in the cross, piercing the silence.

Yes, it is good Friday. In the midst of all the grief and mourning, there is sweet consolation. We are together, and there is love pouring out from our broken hearts and from the pierced heart of God.

HENRI J. M. NOUWEN, *THE SABBATICAL JOURNEY*

THE DEATH OF JESUS

From noon on, darkness came over the whole land until three in the afternoon. And about three o'clock Jesus cried with a loud voice, "Eli, Eli, lema sabachthani?" that is, "My God, my God, why have you forsaken me?" When some of the bystanders heard it, they said, "This man is calling for Elijah." At once one of them ran and got a sponge, filled it with sour wine, put it on a stick, and gave it to him to drink. But the others said, "Wait, let us see whether Elijah will come to save him." Then Jesus cried again with a loud voice and breathed his last. At that moment the curtain of the temple was torn in two, from top to bottom. The earth shook, and the rocks were split. The tombs also were opened, and many bodies of the saints who had fallen asleep were raised.

MATTHEW 27:45–52

PRAYER

God of all beginnings and endings, whose Son is your blessed image and who was nailed to the cross and crucified this day, let me nail my sins to your cross so that they may die with you. Like the Good Thief, let me pray: "Jesus, Son of God, remember me when you come into your kingdom." Amen.

LENTEN ACTION

Observe Good Friday, or Great Friday, as those in the Eastern churches refer to it, by preparing and eating Hot Cross Buns. Alternately, or in addition, prepare a soup with cabbage, lentils, and vinegar for Good Friday supper in honor of the sponge tinged with gall offered to Jesus on the cross.

DAY 46

Holy Saturday

BEING RESURRECTED

*M*ost of the day I spent preparing...for the Easter Vigil celebration....After the Gospel reading I reflected on the significance of our faith in the resurrection of the body. As a community of people conscious of our disabilities [at L'Arche Daybreak], we are held together not so much by the Word as by the body....It is the weak bodies of our core members that create community. We wash, shave, comb, dress, clean, feed, and hold the bodies of those who are entrusted to us and thus build a communal body. As we claim our faith in the resurrection of the body, we come to see that the resurrection is not simply an event after death but a reality of everyday life. Our care for the body calls us to unity...to intimacy...and to integrity.

HENRI J. M. NOUWEN, *THE SABBATICAL JOURNEY:*
THE DIARY OF HIS FINAL YEAR

NAILED TO THE CROSS

In him [Christ Jesus] also you were circumcised with a spiritual circumcision, by putting off the body of the flesh in the circumcision of Christ; when you were buried with him in baptism, you were also raised with him through faith in the power of God, who raised him from the dead. And when you were dead in trespasses and the uncircumcision of your flesh, God made you alive together with him, when he forgave us all our trespasses, erasing the record that stood against us with its legal demands. He set this aside, nailing it to the cross.

COLOSSIANS 2:11–14

PRAYER

God of eternal wisdom, hear my call for help as I keep watch with Christ's disciples at his tomb. Inspire me, as you did Joseph of Arimathea, to find a place of burial for my Lord. I wait in anticipation for the Easter light to deliver me from the darkness of my sins. Amen.

LENTEN ACTION

Mary, the steadfast one, stayed with her Son even through the sorrowful events of the crucifixion. Meditate on the melancholy occurrences of our Mother Mary's life on this day of silent waiting.

PART II

~~~~~~

READINGS *for* EASTER

DAY 47

Easter Sunday

HE IS RISEN!

*E*aster morning. A very simple, quiet Eucharist around the table in Madame Vanier's dining room....A small group of friends happy to be together.

We spoke together about the resurrection. Liz, who works with many anguished people, said, "We have to keep rolling away the large stones that prevent people from coming out of their graves." Elizabeth, who lives with four handicapped people...said, "After the resurrection Jesus had breakfast again with his friends and showed them the importance of the small, ordinary things of life." Sue...said, "It is such a comfort to know that Jesus' wounds remain visible in his risen body. Our wounds are not taken away, but become sources of hope to others."

HENRI J. M. NOUWEN,
THE ROAD TO DAYBREAK: A SPIRITUAL JOURNEY

CHRIST RISES AND DIES NO MORE

Do you not know that all of us who have been baptized into Christ Jesus were baptized into his death? Therefore we have been buried with him by baptism into death, so that, just as Christ was raised from the dead by the glory of the Father, so we too might walk in the newness of life.

For if we have been united with him in a death like his, we will certainly be united with him in a resurrection like his. We know that our old self was crucified with him so that the body of sin might be destroyed, and we might no longer be enslaved to sin. For whoever has died is freed from sin. But if we have died with Christ, we believe that we will also live with him.

ROMANS 6:3–8

PRAYER

God of never-failing light, you who created the bright lights of the sky, you who have no hint of darkness, grant that your flame of hope will renew my intention to serve you and to inflame and purify my actions with your love and mercy. Amen.

EASTER ACTION

Observe this great day with prayers of thanksgiving and with actions symbolizing the significance of our salvation. Wear white on this joyful day in honor of your baptism and in memory of this verse from Revelation: "They stood before the throne and before the Lamb. They wore white robes and held palm branches in their hands—(7:9). Spend some time by candlelight this day in honor of the paschal candle that is lit from the Easter Vigil fire and carried into the church to the words "Christ our Light." Or you may wish to create Easter baskets for the poor and needy.

DAY 48

Monday of Easter Week

PRAY FOR ONE ANOTHER

We often wonder what we can do for others....It is not a sign of powerlessness when we say: "We must pray for one another." To pray for one another is, first of all, to acknowledge, in the presence of God, that we belong to each other as children of the same God. Without this acknowledgment of human solidarity, what we do for one another does not flow from who we truly are....

To pray, that is, to listen to the voice of the One who calls us his "Beloved," is to learn that that voice excludes no one. Where I dwell, God dwells with me and where God dwells with me I find all my sisters and brothers.

HENRI J. M. NOUWEN, *HERE AND NOW: LIVING IN THE SPIRIT*

ABRAHAM AND SARAH

Abraham journeyed toward the region of the Negeb.... While residing in Gerar as an alien, Abraham said of his wife Sarah, "She is my sister." And King Abimelech of Gerar sent and took Sarah. But God came to Abimelech in a dream by night, and said to him, "You are about to die because of the woman whom you have taken; for she is a married woman." Now Abimelech had not approached her; so he said, "Lord, will you destroy an innocent people? Did he not himself say to me, 'She is my sister'? And she herself said, 'He is my brother.' I did this in the integrity of my heart....Then God said to him in the dream, "Yes, I know that you did this in the integrity of your heart; furthermore it was I who kept you from sinning against me.... Now then, return the man's wife; for he is a prophet, and he will pray for you and you shall live."

GENESIS 20:1–7

PRAYER

God of all, I am on this journey of life which is a cycle of life to life: I am born, I live, I die to be born to eternal life. As I pass through on this journey, let my own sinful self die and a new person rise to the challenges of praising you. I will keep the words of the liturgy ever in mind this Eastertide: "Christ has died, Christ is risen, Christ will come again." Amen.

EASTER ACTION

The word liturgy means "work of the people." Make a list of why the celebration of the Sunday liturgy is the most significant event of the week. You might take this opportunity to write a special thank you to the ministers of your parish.

Tuesday of Easter Week

LISTEN TO THE CHURCH

I know that [listening to the Church] isn't a popular bit of advice at a time and in a country where the Church is often seen more as an obstacle in the way than as the way to Jesus. Nevertheless, I'm deeply convinced that the greatest spiritual danger for our times is the separation of Jesus from the Church. The Church is the body of the Lord. Without Jesus there can be no church; and without the Church we cannot stay united with Jesus. I've yet to meet anyone who has come closer to Jesus by forsaking the Church. To listen to the Church is to listen to the Lord of the Church.

Specifically, this entails taking part in the Church's liturgical life. Advent, Christmas, Lent, Easter, Ascension, and Pentecost: these seasons and feasts teach you to know Jesus better and better and unite you more and more intimately with the divine life he offers you in the Church.

HENRI J. M. NOUWEN, *LETTERS TO MARC ABOUT JESUS*

ONE BODY

By the grace given to me I say to everyone among you not to think of yourselves more highly than you ought to think, but to think with sober judgment, each according to the measure of faith that God has assigned. For as in one body we have many members, and not all the members have the same function, so we, who are many, are one body in Christ, and individually we are members one of another.

ROMANS 12:3–5

PRAYER

God of all power, you who left me in the freedom of my own human will, let me dispense with what overfills my life and leaves no room for God and his works. Help me to jettison the idolatry of all that I clutch to so tightly: money, family, fame, other people, and so on. Let me roll away the rocks from in front of my own tomb, let me find a world of new possibilities in your joyful resurrection and in the fullness of your love. Amen.

EASTER ACTION

Now is not the time to be dismal. Smile at all those you meet today.

DAY 50

Wednesday of Easter Week

BEING DISCIPLES

*T*o follow Christ means to relate to each other with the mind of Christ; that is, to relate to each other as Christ did to us—in servanthood and humility. Discipleship is walking together on the same path. While still living wholly *in* this world, we have discovered each other as fellow travelers on the same path and have formed a new community....We have become a new people with a new mind, a new way of seeing and hearing, and a new hope because of our common fellowship with Christ. Compassion, then, can never be separated from community. Compassion always reveals itself in community, in a new way of being together.

HENRI J. M. NOUWEN, DONALD P. MACNEILL,
AND DOUGLAS A. MORRISON,
COMPASSION: A REFLECTION ON THE CHRISTIAN LIFE

OUR HEARTS WERE BURNING IN US

Now on that same day two [disciples] were going to a village called Emmaus, about seven miles from Jerusalem, and talking with each other about all these things that had happened. While they were talking and discussing, Jesus himself came near and went with them, but their eyes were kept from recognizing him....

As they came near the village to which they were going, he walked ahead as if he were going on. But they urged him strongly, saying, "Stay with us, because it is almost evening and the day is now nearly over." So he went in to stay with them. When he was at the table with them, he took bread, blessed and broke it, and gave it to them. Then their eyes were opened, and they recognized him; and he vanished from their sight. They said to each other, "Were not our hearts burning within us while he was talking to us on the road, while he was opening the scripture to us?" That same hour they got up and returned to Jerusalem.

LUKE 24:13–16, 28–33

PRAYER

Great God of the entire human family, give me the ability to recognize Jesus in all whom I meet. Help me to give up my self-centered blindness and open my eyes so that I can acknowledge that we all are one in you. Amen.

EASTER ACTION

Think back and meditate on when you may have "passed by" our Lord as did the disciples on the road to Emmaus.

DAY 51

Thursday of Easter Week

PRECIOUS WAITING

*L*ife is…a short moment of waiting. But life is not empty waiting. It is to wait full of expectation. The knowledge that God will indeed fulfill the promise to renew everything, and will offer us a "new heaven and a new earth," makes the waiting exciting….

This "little while" is a precious time. It is a time of purification and sanctification, a time to be prepared for the great passage to the permanent house of God. What is my task during my "little while"? I want to point to the signs of the Kingdom to come, to speak about the first rays of the day of God, to witness to the many manifestations of the Holy Spirit among us.

HENRI J. M. NOUWEN, *THE SABBATICAL JOURNEY:*
A DIARY OF HIS FINAL YEAR

SORROW BECOMES JOY

*Jesus said: "A little while, and you will no longer see me,
and again a little while and you will see me." Then some of
his disciples said to one another, "What does he mean by...
this 'a little while'...? We do not know what he is talking
about." Jesus knew that they wanted to ask him, so he said
to them.... "Very truly, I tell you, you will weep and mourn,
but the world will rejoice; you will have pain, but your pain
will turn to joy....So you have pain now; but I will see you
again, and your hearts will rejoice, and no one will take
your joy from you."*

JOHN 16:16–18, 20, 22

PRAYER

Eternal Father, Son, and Holy Spirit, though I am here for
"a little while," keep me ever aware that my earthly weep-
ing and mourning will be replaced by rejoicing when I
see you in your heavenly glory. Amen.

EASTER ACTION

Give up nursing grief over past mistakes and instead find
a reason to plan and participate in one joyful celebration.

Friday of Easter Week

EXPERIENCE GOD AS PRESENCE AND ABSENCE

In prayer, God's presence is never separated from God's absence and God's absence is never separated from God's presence. The presence of God is so much beyond the human experience of being together that it quite easily is perceived as absence. The absence of God, on the other hand, is often so deeply felt that it leads to a new sense of God's presence. This is powerfully expressed in Psalm 22. ["My God, my God, why have you forsaken me?"]

This prayer not only is the expression of the experience of the people of Israel, but also the culmination of the Christian experience. When Jesus spoke these words on the cross, total aloneness and full acceptance touched each other. In that moment of complete emptiness all was fulfilled. In that hour of darkness new light was seen. While death was witnessed, life was affirmed.

HENRI J. M. NOUWEN, *REACHING OUT:*
THE THREE MOVEMENTS OF THE SPIRITUAL LIFE

DELIVERANCE

My God, my God, why have you forsaken me?
Why are you so far from helping me,
from the words of my groaning?
O my God, I cry by day, but you do not answer;
and by night, but find no rest.

Yet you are holy,
enthroned on the praises of Israel.
In you our ancestors trusted;
they trusted, and you delivered them.
To you they cried, and were saved;
in you they trusted, and were not put to shame.

But I am a worm, and not human;
scorned by others, and despised by the people.
All who see me mock at me;
they make mouths at me, they shake their heads;
"Commit your cause to the LORD; let him deliver—
let him rescue the one in whom he delights!"...

I am poured out like water,
and all my bones are out of joint;
my heart is like wax;
it is melted within my breast;
my mouth is dried up like a potsherd,
and my tongue sticks to my jaws;
you lay me in the dust of death.

For dogs are all around me;
a company of evildoers encircles me.
My hands and feet have shriveled;
I can count all my bones.

They stare and gloat over me;
they divide my clothes among themselves,
and for my clothing they cast lots.

PSALM 22:1–8, 16–18

PRAYER

God of presence and absence, I know that no matter if I feel your nearness or remoteness, you have never forsaken me. I, however, have alienated you through sin. Somehow I hope that these sins will not be fruitless, but will be transformed through your forgiveness. Amen.

EASTER ACTION

Collect small stones for each person whom you need to forgive. Keep these stones in your pocket or purse as reminders of your intent to seek and grant forgiveness. Remember an old Welsh proverb: "Love flows out of every act of forgiveness."

DAY 53

Saturday of Easter Week

BE JOYFUL

Somehow joy is much harder to express than sadness. It seems that we have more words for sickness than for health, more for abnormal conditions than for normal conditions. Does this mean there is less joy in life than sadness? Perhaps. But it is also possible that joy is in fact a deeper, more intimate, more "normal" condition than sadness and pain, and therefore harder to articulate.

For Jesus, joy is clearly a deeper and more truthful state of life than sorrow. He promises joy as the sign of new life....

Jesus connects joy with the promise of seeing him again. In this sense, it is similar to the joy we experience when a dear friend returns after a long absence. But Jesus makes it clear that joy is more than that. It is "his own joy," flowing from the love he shares with his heavenly Father and leading to completion.

HENRI J. M. NOUWEN, *LIFESIGNS:*
INTIMACY, FECUNDITY, AND ECSTASY IN CHRISTIAN PERSPECTIVE

TRUE JOY

Jesus said: "I am the vine, you are the branches. Those who abide in me and I in them bear much fruit, because apart from me you can do nothing. Whoever does not abide in me is thrown away like a branch and withers; such branches are gathered, thrown into the fire, and burned. If you abide in me, and my words abide in you, ask for whatever you wish, and it will be done for you....As the Father has loved me, so I have loved you; abide in my love. If you keep my commandments, you will abide in my love, just as I have kept my Father's commandments and abide in his love. I have said these things to you so that my joy may be in you, and that your joy may be complete."

JOHN 15:5–11

PRAYER

Loving God, our Father, let my life be a witness to your commandments, let me not be as a withered branch that is thrown into the fire and burned. May I pray to you in joy and in times of adversity. Amen.

EASTER ACTION

No greater gift of love could be demonstrated than the death of our Lord on the cross in reparation for our sins. Perhaps then Eastertide is a better occasion for giving gifts than Christmas. In celebration of Christ's resurrection, give small gifts of commemoration.

DAY 54

Second Sunday of Easter

LISTEN TO YOUR HEART

*I*t's there [in your heart] that Jesus speaks most intimately to you. Praying is first and foremost listening to Jesus who dwells in the very depths of your heart. He doesn't shout. He doesn't thrust himself upon you. His voice is an unassuming voice, very nearly a whisper, the voice of a gentle love. Whatever you do with your life, go on listening to the voice of Jesus in your heart. This listening must be an active and very attentive listening, for in our restless and noisy world Jesus' loving voice is easily drowned out.

HENRI J. M. NOUWEN, *LETTERS TO MARC ABOUT JESUS*

LIVING WATER

On the last day of the festival, the great day, while Jesus was standing there, he cried out, "Let anyone who is thirsty come to me, and let the one who believes in me drink. As the scripture has said, 'Out of the believer's heart shall flow rivers of living water.'"

JOHN 7:37–39

PRAYER

Glorious God, I remember how Moses parted the waters of the Red Sea in order to save the Israelites, I remember how Christ walked on water on the Sea of Galilee, I say with the psalmist, "I truly am thirsty for you, my God." Let these examples and all the oceans, lakes, rivers, creeks, and streams remind me of the goodness of your grace. Amen.

EASTER ACTION

Practice attentive "listening" to your own thoughts. Challenge each and every unkind and angry thought that contaminates your mind.

$\mathscr{S}$ources and $\mathscr{A}$cknowledgments

"I have slowly become aware...," p. 2, *¡Gracias! A Latin American Journal*, copyright © 1983 by Henri J. M. Nouwen. Reprinted by permission of HarperCollins Publishers, Inc.

"Discipline in the spiritual life...," p. 4, *Bread for the Journey: A Daybook of Wisdom and Faith*, copyright © 1996 by Henri J. M. Nouwen. Reprinted by permission of HarperCollins Publishers, Inc.

"We modern Westerners...," p. 6, *Thomas Merton: Contemplative Critic*, copyright © 1981 by Henri J. M. Nouwen. Used by permission of HarperCollins Publishers, Inc.

"I am certainly not ready," p. 8, *Sabbatical Journey: The Diary of His Final Year*, copyright © 1997 by Henri J. M. Nouwen. Used by permission of The Crossroad Publishing Company.

"There is a twilight zone in," p. 10, *Bread for the Journey: A Daybook of Wisdom and Faith*, copyright © 1996 by Henri J. M. Nouwen. Reprinted by permission of HarperCollins Publishers, Inc.

"The word courage comes from," p. 12, *Sabbatical Journey: The Diary of His Final Year*, copyright © 1997 by Henri J. M. Nouwen. Used by permission of The Crossroad Publishing Company.

"This morning during my hour," p. 14, *The Road to Daybreak: A Spiritual Journey*, copyright © 1988 by Henri J. M. Nouwen. Used by permission of Doubleday, a division of Random House, Inc.

"To forgive another person," p. 16, *Bread for the Journey: A Daybook of Wisdom and Faith*, copyright © 1996 by Henri J. M. Nouwen. Reprinted by permission of HarperCollins Publishers, Inc.

"Jesus told people not to be," p. 18, *The Inner Voice of Love: A Journey Through Anguish to Freedom*, copyright © 1996 by Henri J. M. Nouwen. Used by permission of Doubleday, a division of Random House, Inc.